A Miraculous Encounter

by Marcel Jonte'

Copyright © 2021
Marcel Jonte' Gadsden A Miraculous Encounter by Marcel Jonte'
Published by Marcel Jonte'

ISBN: 9798733820347

https://www.jpkb.org/marceljonte (English)
https://marceljonte.amebaownd.com/ (日本語)

marceljonte@gmail.com

Cover Designed by Marcel Jonte'
Building photo created by montypeter - www.freepik.com
Love burger photo by Marcel Jonte'
About Author photo by Chiaki Gadsden

Table of Contents

Your worth is not measured by whether you succeed or fail, nor by the talents and abilities you may or may not have. Not even by whether you are accepted or rejected by people. Your worth is only determined the by One. The One who Loves you and accepts you completely and eternally–your Heavenly Father. Allow that reality to change your life.

–Marcel Jonte'

Prologue: The Encounter

I had an encounter with God I will never forget. It's called a 'Christophany'. Which means a manifestation of Christ. Like Paul shared with the Corinthian church in 2 Corinthians 12, I don't know if I was in my body or outside my body, awake or sleep, but all I know is that I had a real encounter that changed my life. During my early 20's I struggled with anxiety and negative thoughts that blocked me from experiencing the fullness of my new found relationship with God the Father through Jesus Christ.

I was a Christian, but hadn't yet experienced the Christ I was believing in. I would worry and be so consumed with negativity and feelings of shame and condemnation from my mistakes to the point of getting physically sick. These feelings were actually rooted in being bullied and from feelings of rejection I carried as a child. These lies in my mind that kept me bound were called strongholds. A stronghold is a very large fortified castle made to keep enemies from breaching through as seen in the image below.

Spiritually speaking strongholds are walls of negativity that block what is really true about you. It's the habitual pattern of thoughts and feelings that

develop over time and becomes a part of you. I unknowingly looked at all my mistakes as my identity. I internalized every negative experience which made the stronghold even stronger and unbreakable. Each time we entertain a negative thought the stronghold gets taller and thicker blocking out the voice of God which is the truth.

My stronghold was rejection which birthed shame and depression. I felt I could never measure up to God's standards. The problem was I didn't see clearly who God was and who I was in Him. I was totally lost in my own world of negativity until one day I had an experience that served to be the prophetic message to me which led me towards the freedom I now walk in today.

The Christophany

I ascended into Heaven and stood on what seemed like a white cloud. It was all white with a tint of baby blue around the atmosphere and there next to me stood Jesus. He was tall and wore a white robe. I couldn't see his face but at the same time I recognized who he was. I remember jumping up and down for joy next to him.

What amazed me the most was when I was standing next to Jesus I couldn't think of anything negative at all. It was incredible. He was so pure and righteous and so full of all things good that nothing dark could be in his presence. I remember trying to think of the most terrible bad thought I could imagine, but nothing could surface. I couldn't have not one negative thought at all. It was impossible.

I shouted for joy at that fact and expressed my excitement to Jesus. He just stood and was silent. Even though he was silent I could hear his voice and feel his love for me in such a powerful way. I later got a revelation about the meaning of this encounter. Jesus is the truth. When you are close to Jesus you are close to the truth.

"For I am the way, the truth and the life." John 14:6. No lie nor negativity can exist in his presence. Jesus is the spoken word of God. He didn't speak in the encounter because he already had spoken in his word-the very word that you and I both possess. The Bible; God's Word! The strongholds of negativity can only be destroyed by truth.

We all have negative experiences we can never forget. Those experiences shape our complexes, proclivities, negative thought habits and our reactions toward life itself. The reason for writing this book was to expose the lies about yourself and towards the Heavenly Father that will provide you revelation and guide you into a miraculous encounter. Your encounter awaits!

Application:
While reading this book, allow the Holy Spirit to challenge any negative thought patterns. He will work to expose the lies and replace them with the truth.

Scripture:
2 Corinthians 10:4-5 " (For the weapons of our warfare are not carnal, but mighty through God to the pulling down of strong holds;)
5 Casting down imaginations, and every high thing that exalteth itself against the knowledge of God, and bringing into captivity every thought to the obedience of Christ;"

Pray this now:
Father, I pray for an encounter with you through this book. Speak to me and destroy any strongholds in my life. In Jesus name, Amen.

1

Out With The Old In With The New

Before we start taking the journey towards encountering God, we must first understand God's nature in comparison with the Old Testament and the New Testament. Many people struggle with this understanding because all they see in the Old Testament is an angry and strict God. As I'm writing this section of the book, I am sitting at a local restaurant on a sunny Thursday morning. Sitting by this window watching the cars pass by, the brightness of the sun is piercing through with incredible heat and brightness. Although the sunlight is a blessing it's just too bright and hot to really enjoy what I'm doing.

So I had to pull down the blinds. This is an example of the Old Testament and the New Testament. In the Old Testament Jesus wasn't fully revealed as the Son of God so God wasn't recognized as the Heavenly Father yet. In other words, in the

Old Testament people had to come into direct contact with the burning brightness of the sunlight of God's holiness without any blinds. That can be unbearable.

When Moses came down the mountain after 40 days with God constructing the 10 commandments he had to wear a veil to cover his face due to the bright glory of God. Imagine yourself standing in front of the actual sun. Research shows that the Sun is 3.5 Million degrees fahrenheit or 2 million degrees celsius. That's very hot! Therefore, it's dangerous and nearly impossible to stand in front of the burning sun. So it was to stand before a holy God in the Old Testament.

In the Old Testament there was nothing to cover the sinfulness of man in the presence of a holy and pure God. That's why it seemed God was mean or strict. It's not that God was mean or strict. It's the mire fact that he is Holy. God's nature is Holy.

Holy means without spot or blemish. No unrighteousness can stand in his presence. In the same way we cannot stand before the sun without getting burned. That's why in the Old Testament God required priests to atone for the sins of the people through the sacrifice of an unblemished animal to represent a holy sacrifice on their behalf because they nor we were without blemish. So, God's nature is Holy, not strict or mean. Now when Christ was revealed in the New Testament as the Son of God, Christ stood between sinful man and the Holy God.

"For there is one God, and one mediator between God and men, the man Christ Jesus;" 1 Timothy 2:5. Thats why all throughout the New Testament Jesus spoke of his Father. He came to glorify the Father and reveal him to us. He came to wash us of sin and to present us faultless before God in love. Hallelujah! Christ Jesus was like those blinds that reduced the heat and brightness of the Sun for me at the restaurant.

Now with Christ in the middle we can have a relationship with the Holy Heavenly Father and be presented before him without spot or blemish in his sight. God made it possible through Christ for us to be accepted into the family of God though we were sinners. What a powerful demonstration of his love for you and for me!

Application:
See God as your Heavenly Father and Jesus as your mediator between you and God. Replace any thoughts of pressure and fear towards God with the scriptures below.

Scriptures:
Jude 1:24 "Now unto him (Christ) that is able to keep you from falling, and to present you faultless before the presence of his glory with exceeding joy,"
John 17:4 "I have glorified thee (Father) on the earth: I have finished the work which thou gavest me to do."

Pray this now:
Father, open my heart to see you as I'm supposed to see you. Remove from my heart all negative thoughts I have about you and reveal your love through Jesus to me. In Jesus name, Amen.

2

Dinner Time

Although I've never met the builders who built the house I'm living in, I never doubt that builders built it. When I fly on an airplane I never doubt that someone is flying the plane although I've never seen nor met the pilot. To take it a little further, although I've never seen my great ancestors before, I never doubt their existence because my existence is proof of their existence. However we often seem to doubt the existence and the presence of the One who created us and the world we live in.

"The god of this world hath blinded the minds of them which believe not, lest the light of the glorious gospel of Christ, who is the image of God, should shine unto them "2 Corinthians 4:4. The enemy seeks to plant doubt in our minds because he knows the Kingdom of God is accessed by faith. Not like the world where sight is the measure of reality. The reality of the Kingdom of God and of the Heavenly

Father must be accessed by and through faith. Doubt comes from the spirit of fear.

This is a spirit that 2 Timothy 1:7 says God didn't give us. Fear says, "what if". What "IF" means "i fear". I fear my life is nothing. I fear it's all for nothing. I fear I have no real value or worth.

I fear God doesn't love me. I fear I'm not really forgiven, etc. The spirit of fear tells us to run out and seek answers through pleasure, money, false security in people, and a myriad of other things. Jesus said in Matthew 6:25-33, Take no thought for what you will eat or wear because your Heavenly Father already knows what you need before you even think to ask him. Therefore the underlying problem is not that the Father doesn't know what we need, it's that we don't really know the Father.

"Fear not, little flock; for it is your Father's good pleasure to give you the kingdom." Luke 12:32. Not knowing the Father makes us live in constant fear. You will be surprised to know the opposite of love is not hate. It is fear. "There is no fear in love; but perfect love casteth out fear: because fear hath torment. He that feareth is not made perfect in love." 1 John 4:18.

Imagine you're a kid running down the street knocking on every door in the neighborhood begging for food. All the while your father is home preparing dinner. Why would you still go out and beg? There are only two explanations to why a child would do that. One is that your father is abusive and you fear going home to eat with him or you simply doubt your father is even home preparing dinner at all.

If the second explanation is true something is wrong with the child's view and understanding of the father. There had to be some kind of trauma this child went through to make him not trust the father who is home preparing dinner. The father is neither neglectful nor abusive. It's the child that doesn't yet believe in the Love of the father who is at home preparing dinner. Fear sets in and makes the child seek out and struggle on his own. It's an orphan mentality.

The children of Israel witnessed the greatest miracle ever recorded in the Bible when God delivered them from 400 years of slavery in Egypt. They escaped Egypt's captivity, left with provisions and crossed over the big Red Sea on dry land. Then God brought them to a new place of living. You would think they would be ok and feel safe.

But the truth is though they were free from Egypt's oppression physically they were still captive emotionally and spiritually to the bonds that enslaved them. The Father was "preparing dinner for them in the house" and yet and still they doubted him over and over again. Fear. When we come to Christ, God frees us from our old life of fear, disappointments, and uncertainties by (including) us in the family of God. You are not excluded. You are included.

God becomes our father, our protector and our source. However though free, we tend to act like we don't have a Heavenly Father at all and begin to be anxious, worried and depressed about life totally forgetting that the Father knows the plan for us. He's preparing dinner. Stay in the house and trust him.

Application:
It's time to let go the spirit of fear that has gripped you. It's time to be released from all binding thoughts of doubt and unbelief of the Heavenly Father's love for you.

Scripture:
Romans 8:15 "For ye have not received the spirit of bondage again to fear; but ye have received the Spirit of adoption, whereby we cry, Abba, Father."

Pray this now:
In the name of Jesus, Lord remove the stronghold of fear that has caused me to doubt your unfailing love for me. I want to be free! Renew my mind to think on things that only come from you in Jesus name Amen!

3

Good Boy!

I remember getting ready to go to church one Sunday when I was about 15 years old when my dad asked me to go outside and move something for him. I was already in my church clothes–all dressed up. So I decided not to wear my dress shoes to do the chore to prevent them from getting dirty. I removed those shoes and put on my old sneakers. When I finished what my dad asked me to do, I ran in and told him I was done and how I didn't wear my good shoes but wore my old shoes. I can never forget how he made me feel when he said, "Good boy Marcel!"

A surge of joy and a sense of self worth overwhelmed me making me smile ear to ear. I felt I had worth because of what my dad said to me. This had to be the first time my dad ever said this to me since I could remember. From that moment the strict and at times hard dad I was accustomed to seeing became nice and loving in my eyes. How could anyone reject me if my dad said "Good Boy Marcel!" to me? Impossible.

His words carried a lot of weight. My love for him at that moment changed. I felt accepted by him. This memory still remains with me today. I often recount that day and what I felt because it's a perfect picture of what we all long for in life.

The 5 basic needs that every person seeks and longs for are as follows:

1. Affirmation
2. Attention
3. Appreciation
4. Acceptance
5. Affection

These 5 basic needs our Heavenly daddy has bestowed on us. We have received *Affirmation* from God, We have God's total *Attention*, We are *Appreciated* by God, We are *Accepted* by God and we are the center of his *Affection* and receive affection from him.

Take a look at each of these points outlined in scripture.

1.) Affirmed By God *(What he says about me)*

"Nay, in all these things we are more than conquerors through him that loved us." Romans 8:37

2.) We Have God's Attention

(How he cares about me)

"But even the very hairs of your head are all numbered. Fear not therefore: ye are of more value than many sparrows." Luke 12:7

3.) We Are Appreciated By God

(How he feels about me)

"That we should be to the praise of his glory, who first trusted in Christ." Ephesians 1:12

4.) We Are Accepted By God

(How he acts towards me)

"To the praise of the glory of his grace, wherein he hath made us accepted in the beloved." Ephesians 1:6

5.) Center of His Affection

(How he connects with me)

"But he that is joined unto the Lord is one spirit."
1 Corinthians 6:17

The difference between your dad, this world, and your Heavenly Father

Recount the ministry of Jesus and how it started. Jesus didn't just go out and start healing and helping people right away. Something happened before that. He was affirmed first. Affirmation of a child comes from the father while the mother provides nurturing to the child.

The words of a father to a child are words and actions that provide a child a sense of identity. This is true for all people of the world no matter your race or culture. So, after Jesus was baptized by John the Baptist the Bible records that the heavens were open and a voice came from heaven saying "This is my beloved son, in whom I'm well pleased." Now this is different from what my dad did and from what the world as we know it does. After I finished the chore my dad affirmed me. Right?

When you go to work and perform good works you are rewarded with a salary. The applause comes after the show in other words. Those affirming words "Good boy Marcel!" my dad said to me that day though it was so comforting cannot compare with how our Heavenly Father affirms us. He operates differently. Our Heavenly Father affirms us (before) we ever do anything good.

That's a total game changer. That's a total paradigm shift. He does this to assure you of your identity and worth that it's grounded in Him and not in your works. So when God the Father opened up the heavens and spoke to Jesus and affirmed him, he affirmed his identity as his son and told him (before) he did any good works on the earth that he was pleased with him. Could you imagine the courage and power you would have in your life if you knew already every morning when you woke up that the Father was pleased with you?

That would change how you act. It would change how you react to people. That understanding would change your attitude about your life because your identity is not based on what you do. Your identity would be based on what the Father said. His words of affirmation and validation would influence your actions for good works.

If you know that he is pleased with you already before you do anything, you will by nature do good because your Father is good and he says you are good so because the Father affirms you, you will act in alignment to what the Father says about you. And if you do wrong, the loving Father is full of grace to forgive you when you confess to him. His position of love for you doesn't change based on any circumstance. It's truly unconditional love. Your faith in Jesus gives you that access to the forgiveness and justification found in The Heavenly Father. The Heavenly Father says Good boy! and good girl! to you today!

Application:

See yourself already pleasing to the Father. Stop looking at your faults, your performance and works. Those come naturally as you see yourself the way the Father sees you–His beloved Son/Daughter in whom he is well pleased.

Scriptures:

Ephesians 2:8-9 "For by grace are ye saved through faith; and that not of yourselves: it is the gift of God: Not of works, lest any man should boast."
1 John 1:9 "If we confess our sins, he is faithful and just to forgive us our sins, and to cleanse us from all unrighteousness."

Pray this now:

Father, open my eyes to see you. Open my heart to see myself as you see me. I believe I am affirmed by you, I have your total attention, that I am appreciated by you, accepted by you, and that I am the center of your affection. Help me to see this clearer and clearer each day. In Jesus name, Amen.

4

The Love Burger

I have to admit I love hamburgers. In fact mostly everywhere I eat I look for a good burger. So, when I think about God's love it helps me understand it as if I am ordering a nice juicy burger. I'll explain. 1 Corinthians chapter 13 is famous for outlining what God's love is like. This scripture is used in wedding vows around the world and is the cornerstone of what we understand about God's love. For example it says how love is patience, kind, and not prideful etc. However I will sum up all of what 1 Corinthians 13 says about love into 4 major points. I call this the Love Burger. It's not enough to know about a good burger you've got to experience it! Let's begin with the bun on the top!

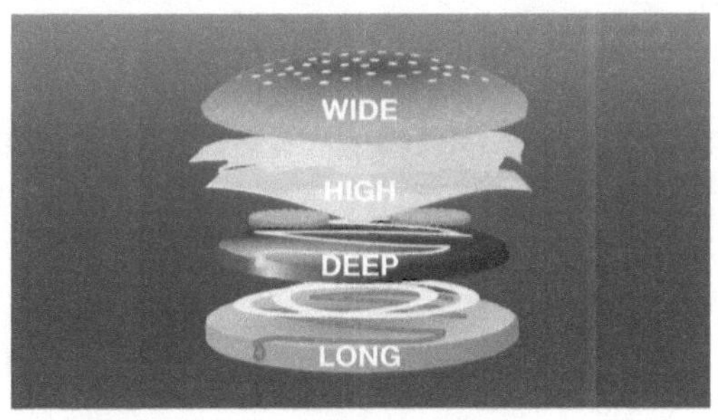

1. God's love is wide enough to be everywhere

Then let's add some lettuce & Cheese

2. God's love is high to overlook our sins

Let's move on to the meat

3. God's love is deep enough to reach us

Lastly, the bottom bun

4. God's love is long enough to last forever

These four characteristics of God's limitless love is from Ephesians 3:18-19 which says "May be able to comprehend with all saints what is the breadth, and length, and depth, and height; 19And to know the love of Christ, which passeth knowledge, that ye might be filled with all the fullness of God. Can you see the burger? Once you eat this burger you will be filled with all the fullness of God! Delightful! When someone experiences the Love of the Father their lives totally change.

The following are outcomes of experiencing the Love of the Father:

<u>1. You become more confident in yourself.</u>
When you know you are loved beyond limit you will live with incredible confidence. Our fears and insecurities are directly linked to how we feel about ourselves. Knowing how God the Father feels about you will free you to take steps of faith even when it looks impossible. You are loved.

<u>2. You become difficult to offend.</u>
This is because if God accepts you who can offend you? "What shall we then say to these things? If God be for us, who can be against us?" Romans 8:31. We live in a world where offenses happen. Not everyone is well mannered and God-fearing so at times you will be mistreated. And when the mistreatment comes it won't define you because you've been accepted by your Heavenly Father. People lose the power to offend you. Hallelujah!

<u>3. You become more bold</u>
Imagine your father was the president of your country. If he were a really nice dad, nothing would stop him from paying attention to you when you needed him. In the same way the Father is never too busy to talk with us and care for us. "Let us therefore come boldly unto the throne of grace, that we may obtain mercy, and find grace to help in time of need." Hebrews 4:16. We are to come boldly before God. Nowhere in the Bible does it say we are to come to God with fancy prayers and big words. Don't

compare how others pray and how you pray. Gods not looking for a set model for prayer. He says just come to me like a child would a father. Boldly. "Hey dad, I need your help."

4. You become more friendly and a lover of people
 "If a man say, I love God, and hateth his brother, he is a liar: for he that loveth not his brother whom he hath seen, how can he love God whom he hath not seen?" 1 John 4:20. To be a Christian that doesn't love people is like going bowling with a pineapple. Something is wrong.

It's important to point out that God doesn't "have" Love. In the same way I don't "have" myself. "I am" Marcel. God "IS" love. So if I have God which is the same as having Love, it should be all but natural for me to love others because God "IS" love. "He that loveth not knoweth not God; for God IS love." 1 John 4:8.

 So if God the Father is the embodiment of Love, what are his true characteristics?

"Love is patient, love is kind. It does not envy, it does not boast, it is not proud. It is not rude, it is not self-seeking, it is not easily angered, it keeps no record of wrongs. Love does not delight in evil but rejoices with the truth. It always protects, always trusts, always hopes, always perseveres. Love never fails."1 Corinthians 13:4-8.

In other words, God IS patience. God IS kind. God IS forgiveness! I should be patient, kind and forgiving towards people too! If you have received him you ought to walk in his nature which is Love. However, at times our past pains, self doubt, regrets, resentments, unforgiveness and bitterness block us from experiencing the Fathers love for ourselves and expressing it to others–blocking what we already have received from God. We have received a nice juicy love burger that tastes great! It's time to eat it!

Application:
Eat the Love burger fully. Receive his Love for you because it's true. God loves you!

Scripture:
1 John 4:19 "We love him, because *he first loved us.*

Pray this now:
Father, free me from anything that may be blocking my reception of your Love. All unforgiveness and resentment I give to you today. I seek your strength to help me let it go. Thank you Father for your limitless Love for me. In Jesus name, Amen.

5

Getting Rid of Worry & Fear

We typically worry about 3 areas in life. Worry about the future, worry about the present and worry about the past. Worry is the first sign of not clearly knowing the Father. If not careful worry can become a stronghold (A habitual mental pattern). I'm guilty at times of allowing worry to creep in because of how easy it is to allow circumstances to push us away from the knowledge of our loving Heavenly Father that cares for us.

That's why we must be reminded of the reality of our relationship with the Father. Jesus outlines to us in Matthew 6 the difference between someone who knows they are their Fathers child and someone who doesn't. The person who doesn't know typically worries. He taught, "Take no thought for your life, what ye shall eat, or what ye shall drink; nor yet for your body, what ye shall put on." He went on to say,

this is the way the "Heathens" behave. In other words, "the people who don't know their Daddy". Don't be like them!
Your Father knows what you have need of before you even begin to ask him. Matthew 6:7-8,25-33. God is sharing with us through the life of Jesus how we are to think and operate as children of God.

The second sign a person doesn't know the Fathers love is Fear. This Includes Panic. We typically fear the following things in life:

- Fear of people
- Fear of failure
- Fear of trying
- Fear of rejection
- Fear of death

Fear is the brother of worry. They both lack trust and faith in God. Normally fears are connected with something much more deeper than meets the surface. Fears are powered by lies and lies build walls. As I explained in Chapter 2, the Bible shares how the opposite of Love is fear.

This scripture freed me from the spirit of fear because it revealed the Love of the Father has the weakness of fear. "There is no fear in love; but perfect love casteth out fear: because fear hath torment. He that feareth is not made perfect in love." 1 John 4:18. We have to become more perfected in the Love of the Father in understanding and in revelation to properly remove the spirit of fear.

Application:
Worry and fear must be removed from your life because you are cared for by your loving Heavenly Father. Allow the truth of those words to give you understanding and freedom. Remember to catch those worry and fearful thoughts each time they surface and recognize them as ways in which the enemy is trying to pull you away from knowing the Love of the Father for you.

Scripture:
1 Peter 5:7 "Give all your worries and cares to God, for he cares about you."

Pray this now:
Father in the name of Jesus, forgive me for walking in worry and fear. Help me to recognize in every situation I face, that I am yours and that you care for me. In Jesus name, Amen.

6

My Turnaround Experience

Unknown to me I had what was called an 'orphan spirit'. Like the analogy I shared previously about the kid who didn't trust that his father was home preparing dinner for him and began to run out to the neighbor's houses begging for food, that kid was me. I was consumed with anxiety, worry and fear of my future. I wasn't sure of anything and lived so stressed out about everything.

I developed pains in my stomach area and would also have heart palpitations due to stress. All because of how I viewed God. I didn't know him as Father. I was in my early 20's when I struggled trying to measure up to the standards of God until I later realized that I didn't have to strive to be perfect because I was already made perfect in my Fathers eyes. It's the difference from having a work mentality vs. a 'rest' mentality.

I was working to be righteous and pleasing to God rather than resting in my faith that I have been justified through the grace of God. Ephesians 2:8,9 "For by grace are ye saved through faith; and that not of yourselves: it is the gift of God: Not of works, lest any man should boast. When you are in a relationship with someone you love and who loves you, you are at rest. In other words you are at peace. You're not trying to win their love and acceptance. You already have . Then from that state of peace comes security.

I didn't feel secure in my relationship with God because of the daunting thoughts of condemnation, shame and the fear of not measuring up. Don't get me wrong, God doesn't approve of sin but until we realize we have been made righteous through the sacrifice of Christ we will continue to act like sinners and fatherless children.

My trip to Baltimore

It was early 2010 when I saw a YouTube video advertisement for an upcoming conference in Baltimore, Maryland called 'Voice of the Apostles' with event host Randy Clark that I felt the Lord was leading me to attend. I was 23 years old and desperately wanted to be used by God here in Japan because of the strong calling I felt. But I didn't know what was awaiting me at this conference. All I felt was that something there was for me. I had to go!

Such awakening, such new revelation and a whole new paradigm shift was awaiting me at that conference. I gathered up some money from my savings and took the trip with a friend from church. We headed to Baltimore, Maryland for this three day life changing conference with some of the most amazing pastors and worship leaders in Christianity to include Randy Clark, Bill Johnson, Heidi Baker, Kim Walker and many more. These three days away from Japan was to say the least–transformative. For the past three days all the messages spoken was on the supernatural power of God and the revelation of the Father's Love.

Everyone present desired to do something for the Kingdom of God. We were all hungry for it. I learned that of course it's important to want to do something to please God with our lives, however how we go about doing it and our mindset is most important.

The position of our hearts and how we see ourselves is vital in order to do anything for God. I remember seeing healings both physical and emotional for the first time in my life. Surgical metal plates and screws in people's bodies were miraculously dissolved and their pains healed, deafness, broken bones, blindness all healed and I also witnessed the healing of the orphan spirit.

Hearing various messages preached about being accepted by God challenged my current view and understanding of God. Because I was brought up by a strict father and all I ever knew was I had to be somewhat a perfect child or risk getting into trouble. I learned that before Jesus did any works, any miracles, or helped anyone he was affirmed by the Father first. Fully validated by the Father–Matthew 3:16-17. The Father gave Jesus his identity as well as affirmed him that he was already pleased with him before he ever did anything.

I didn't understand this fully until the third day of the conference. It was a time of powerful prayer and impartation. I remember seeing hundreds of people crying, praying and feeling something from God but not me. In fact there were many in that room like me who felt nothing. Then as if the speaker understood what we all were feeling, got up on the microphone and said something to the effect of "those of you out there who feel like somethings wrong with you because you're not expressing like the others around you, that is a blatant lie from the enemy."

"The enemy wants you to feel like you're not worthy or that something is wrong with you! Nothing is wrong with you! Just be like a feather in the wind! Don't resist, just flow with him" Those words freed me so much giving me confidence in God-my Father who wanted to bless me and free me. The room was scattered around with everybody praying for one another.

My friend and I joined with a group of people at the back right side of the room. That's where I had my breakthrough. This amazingly nice woman named Margaret who was so filled with the Love of God and friends prayed for me and prophesied over me how the Father approves of me, how I didn't need to hold guilt and shame and condemnation and how the Lord would use me for the nations of the world. I remember feeling a strong surge of joy as I fell to the floor laughing. Spontaneous spiritual laughter!

It was so refreshing. I felt the Father's love for me like I've never had before. So powerful and yet so warm. The Bible talks about joy unspeakable. "Whom having not seen, ye love; in whom, though now ye see him not, yet believing, ye rejoice with joy unspeakable and full of glory:" 1 Peter 1:8.

That's why I was laughing. It was spiritual laughter from my spirit. I was made free! The moment I was released from the thought of feeling rejected I felt the Lord moving in me. I had a miraculous encounter that literally changed my life.

From that day forward my worship toward the Lord changed. That night returning to the hotel I was up all night worshipping the Lord and speaking with him. I couldn't get enough of my Father! So glorious and so freeing. Nothing could shake my encounter with the Father. He was always there the whole time.

It was my mindset and works mentality and feeling like a failure that was blocking my understanding and encounter with him the whole time. I pray for this freedom and encounter for you.

Application:
Never compare other people's expressions with your expressions toward God. They may cry, lift their hands and you not feel anything. That doesn't mean that somethings wrong with you or that God is not blessing you. Instead think of anything that could be blocking you from what the Father has already given you. Perhaps you need to only open up your heart and be like a feather in the wind. Don't resist. Just flow with Him!

Scripture:
1 Peter 1:8 "Whom having not seen, ye love; in whom, though now ye see him not, yet believing, ye rejoice with joy unspeakable and full of glory:"

Pray this now:
Father, I pray in the name of Jesus, that I be released from every care and worry that's trying to keep me from encountering the joy and freedom you have already given me. In Jesus name, Amen.

Your encounter awaits!

About the Author

Marcel Jonte' Having traveled the world, i.e. Europe, North American and Asia through his father's military career, Marcel has become an expert communicator with all nationalities and ages of people and has gained a unique perspective on life, relationships and living your purpose. Moving to Japan in 1999 was a challenge for Marcel as he didn't understand the Japanese culture or the language. However, Marcel challenged himself to learn and later served over ten years as a graphic artist and advertising sales consultant for various companies throughout Tokyo. In 2014 Marcel married his beloved wife Chiaki, and in 2017 they founded their organization Japan Kingdom Builders, Inc.

As Founder and CEO of Japan Kingdom Builders, Inc, Marcel manage and oversee a Kids English Program, Gospel Music Program, an Event Rental Studio and the Akiramenai Homeless Rehabilitation Program. In addition to being a CEO, Marcel also pastors Japan Kingdom Church, where he actively trains and inspires people of various nationalities through his life encouraging messages weekly.

ENGLISH URL:
    http://www.jpkb.org/marceljonte
    http://www.facebook.com/marceljonte
    http://www.facebook.com/japankingdomchurch

JAPANESE URL:
    http://marceljonte.amebaownd.com

More Books By Marcel Jonte

The Reason Why I Am Black - The Love Challenge

What if everyone in your world was just like you? Relationships with people would be a lot easier. However, you know that's fantasy because the reality is your friends, husband, wife, mom, dad, brother, sister, co-workers and or stranger is totally different than you, which can cause disagreements and difficulties at times. In the Reason Why I am Black, Marcel Jonte shares how our differences reveal a clue to understanding what the true meaning of Love is and how it's not limited to those we are familiar with. Here lies the challenge. The Love Challenge.

Be prepared to discover:
* How to live a healthy love-life without limits
* The importance of loving yourself first
* How to develop a forgiving heart
* How to love difficult people and more!

friend, a brother, a sister, a mother, a father or an employee. The love principle works!

I wrote a book called "The reason why I am Black– the Love challenge and it has helped so many people gain a new understanding of what love really is. That's why I decided to make an additional guide to go along with the Love challenge book at no cost to you! Also because the free Love Challenge Guide content is LIFE CHANGING.

www.ingramcontent.com/pod-product-compliance
Lightning Source LLC
Chambersburg PA
CBHW021327160726
47994CB00004B/1648